The Queen's Green Beads

Written by Alison Hawes

Illustrated by Anni Axworthy

Rigby

Three thieves crept
On silent feet.
They met in the moonlight
On an empty street.

Each one looked mean,
And each one was keen
To sneak to the castle
And steal from the queen.

The leader then said,

> What each of us needs
> Is to seek in the castle
> For the queen's green beads.

They glow and gleam
A deep, dark green.
They are kept in the room
That belongs to the queen.

See, here's the map
We need to read.
Just see what it says,
Then follow my lead.

The steep hill where the queen keeps her sheep

The castle where the queen is asleep

The peach tree under the room where the queen sleeps

It will be easy.
Don't speak or scream.
Don't squeal or squeak.
We'll work as a team.

Bleat!

No ear will hear
When we sneak and creep.
We'll reach the castle
While the queen is asleep.

The stream was deep.
The far bank was steep.
They tried to reach it
With one huge leap.

Up to their knees
In mud and weeds,
They began to wonder,
If they'd ever succeed.

They climbed up the tree
And made not a peep.
They were pleased to find
The queen still asleep.

In the queen's bedroom
Was a big steel box,
Where she kept the beads
And which was always locked.

They saw the key
Underneath the feet
Of the queen's much loved
Pet parakeet.

But a creak of the floor
As the first thief reached
To unhook the key
Woke the bird, who screeched.

The screech woke the queen
Who started to shout,
"You can't have my beads.
Now just get out!"

Caught in the act
Of doing the deed,
The thieves disappeared
At lightning speed.
Down the peach tree,
Away from the queen,
And back through the town,
Never more to be seen!